FLASHLIGHT FIGHTING

● ● ● ● ● ●

How to Make Your
Pocket Flashlight
a Take-Anywhere
Self-Defense Weapon

Phil Elmore

PALADIN PRESS • BOULDER, COLORADO

Dedication

For my wife—the light in the darkness.

*Flashlight Fighting: How to Make Your Pocket Flashlight
a Take-Anywhere Self-Defense Weapon*
by Phil Elmore

Copyright © 2006 by Phil Elmore

ISBN 13: 978-1-58160-502-0
Printed in the United States of America

Published by Paladin Press, a division of
Paladin Enterprises, Inc.
Gunbarrel Tech Center
7077 Winchester Circle
Boulder, Colorado 80301 USA
+1.303.443.7250

Direct inquiries and/or orders to the above address.

Visit our Web site at www.paladin-press.com

Table of Contents

Warning

Some of the techniques in this book are dangerous and should not be attempted without the supervision of a certified instructor.

The author, publisher, and distributors of this book disclaim any liability from any damage or injuries of any type that a reader or user of information contained within this book may incur from the use of said information. This book is *for academic study only*.

Special Thanks

No one learns in a vacuum, and everyone learns from others. I'm grateful for those from whom I've learned what I know today, either directly or through their work.

I'd also like to thank everyone who has offered me encouragement, advice, or assistance in the course of my martial journey. Among them—in no particular order—I'd like to thank, first, my wonderful wife, and then David W. Pearson, Dan Donzella, Bob Maucher, Lawrence Keeney, Danny Rowell, Tony Manifold, Don Rearic, Craig Douglas, Kelly Worden, Robert Humelbaugh, John Gillespie, Loren W. Christensen, Dan Webre, Scott Sonnon, Rich Dimitri, Mike Janich, Jerry VanCook, F.S. (maker of the Hideaway Knife), Dwight McLemore, and Ed Lawrence.

Also, Kevin Hinshaw, Dexter Ewing, Jason Panick, Don Roley, Johnny Matarazzo, Marc MacYoung, Alain Burrese, Ted Truscott, Jack Rumbaugh, Gabe Suarez, Barry Eisler, Nick and Frank of CountyComm.com, Harvey Moul, Lyman Wood, Frank Mrozowski, Damir Mehmedic, Ronald Pehr, Vinnie Moscaritolo, Lenny Magill, David Craik, Bram Frank, Rod Bremer, Chris Cashbaugh, Joyce Laituri and Sal Glesser, Jon Ford of Paladin Press, my brother Daryl, my sister Monica, Mom and Dad, the members of *The Martialist*'s online forum, the contributors to *The Martialist* e-zine, and the countless others I've left out in trying and failing to compose a comprehensive list.

My thanks, my apologies, and my best wishes to you all.

www.themartialist.com

Introduction

If you don't have a tactical light, all the other urban warriors will laugh and make fun of you. You will be branded as an incompetent by the tactical establishment. You will wander helplessly, doomed to bark your shins on unseen coffee tables, tripping over any and all objects strewn in your path. You will drop your keys and be unable to find them. You will have no way to read a novel while sitting in your car at night. Black-clad ninja will leap from the shadows at the first opportunity, and you will be powerless in the murky darkness. You will be defeated as you struggle helplessly in the night. You will never be seen again. Your family and friends will be forced to live with the shame of your poorly lighted demise.

OK, now that we've gotten all that silliness out of the way, we can dismiss the equally silly literature that promotes tactical lights as generators of eyeball-searing, blinding pure whiteness that burns assailants dead with a flick of your righteous thumb on a tailcap switch. No, your personal torch will not scatter barbarian hordes with streams of deadly photons. Miscreants will not run before you with tears streaming from their eyes. Would-be muggers will not fall dead, their faces melted by the heat, when you trigger your flashlight in their faces.

Personal lights *are* extremely useful, however. If you do not own a tactical torch, you should. This does not mean such lights are magical wands of pupil-contracting justice. They are, however, yet another means of stacking the odds in your favor in an altercation. In any low-light condition, the ability to put bright light where you want it for the duration of your choosing is a definite advantage. Carrying with you an implement that is stronger than the bones of your hand is also an advantage.

The portable torch is a *weapon*. While plenty of literature exists explaining and demonstrating how to use the portable light as a self-defense accessory—most often in conjunction with a firearm—this book is devoted to the use of the flashlight as a weapon in its own right. While carrying a portable light, you are not simply prepared for utility problems that may arise; you are, in fact, always armed while equipped with such a tool.

Most of the concepts I'll share with you in this book seem to me to be fairly intuitive, but where self-defense is concerned, it never hurts to hear the obvious stated explicitly. The ideas contained in this text form the only primer you'll ever need on tactical lights as self-defense weapons. Combine the concepts written herein with your own study in the martial arts and self-defense and you will be well armed to face adversity. Technology may change, but the principles of light—and of fighting with lighting tools—do not.

Why the Flashlight?

Chapter 1

When I was a boy, my father—an engineer by trade—carried the classic nerd's pocket protector in his shirt pocket. He was never without a pen, a pencil, a small notebook (in which he kept notes, reminders, and the vital statistics of his daily life), and a penlight. A Boy Scout in spirit if not in fact, my father was the most prepared man I've ever known. He carried the biggest Swiss army knife it was possible to buy at the time. He drove around with what was practically a fully equipped machine shop in the back of his truck. It said something to me, therefore, that riding in the place of honor in his shirt pocket was that little light.

There is no denying the utility of a personal light. Thanks to my dad, I always carry a flashlight. I've used it to light the back of my computer and the underside of my desk while untangling cords, to search the corners of hotel rooms to make sure I'm leaving nothing behind or under the bed, to find my way in dimly lighted used bookstores, to search for my car among hundreds of others at night after the state fair, and to comb the floor of my car looking for a lost pocketknife. I've used it to warn off traffic while crossing busy streets at night in Boston and New York. I've also used that light to check home and driveway after suspicious noises.

FLASHLIGHT FIGHTING

During one particularly unnerving incident, my ability to put bright light where I wanted it was all that separated me from the night and an irrational, distraught man screaming obscenities in a parking lot at 3:45 in the morning.

A typical, portable flashlight, also known as a tactical torch.

The flashlight is among the few useful items one may carry that has yet (as of this writing) to be legislated into liability. Guns are strictly controlled in some areas. Knives are subject to as many if not more laws, some of them so vague that they defy interpretation. Collapsible batons, billy clubs, mace, and pepper sprays are often illegal, as are most weapons associated with the Eastern martial arts. Even the possession of a humble pocket stick or yawara—a simple wooden dowel—is restricted in some municipalities. What almost all these locations have in common, however, is that few if any of them regulate the possession of the common pocket torch. You will face enough problems in the aftermath of any act of self-defense, from the potential for prosecution to the inevitable civil lawsuits from criminals "victimized" by your refusal to be beaten or robbed; why make things worse by using a weapon that is considered illegal?

About now you're probably thinking that you're in deep trouble if the only weapon you've got during a self-defense scenario is a battery-powered flashlight. While there are certainly more effective fighting tools—I'd rather have my customized .45 and a Spyderco Civilian folding knife in addition to that light—the torch is an extremely potent weapon if wielded properly. Large flashlights are clubs; small flashlights are used according to palm stick principles (which we'll discuss a little later on). Anyone who knows how to use a palm stick or pocket stick knows just how effective even a short length of rigid material can be. Thrusted into the body's soft targets, joints, and other vital areas, a palm stick can debilitate and even kill an attacker. That's right; I'm telling you that your AA flashlight is a potentially lethal weapon that is legal to carry almost anywhere. That's the point of this book.

There's another reason the flashlight is such a powerful self-defense tool. The obvious function of the portable torch is to provide *light*. Light helps us to see what is unseen. Light dispels fear and exposes deceit. Criminals prefer darkness for the concealment, the anonymity, that a lack of light provides. Psychologically, we as individuals are much less likely to be afraid if we can see what is going on around us.

FLASHLIGHT FIGHTING

Why do you think children often have nightlights and fear their darkened bedrooms? When all we can see is shadows, our minds invent things to fear. Even familiar objects become ominous shapes at night. When our nerves are frayed, our courage often falters. While it is by no means a substitute for true mental and emotional fortitude, light helps immensely in any dim environment. More importantly, those who seek the cover of darkness are less comfortable in the light of day. You cannot carry the sun with you, but some of the portable lights available are the next best thing.

Before you begin considering specific brands and types of lights, you have to choose the general category of light you'll carry. You've seen police officers on television with very large flashlights held overhand. (Consider why you might hold a big light this way; you can easily bring the light down in a clubbing motion.) If you've ever hefted an aluminum-body flashlight filled with three or four D-cell batteries, you know you wouldn't want to be struck in the head with one. When I was a college student our campus security guards carried only multi-D-cell lights on the job, but they were sufficiently armed to do their jobs. The only problem with a big, heavy light is that it is . . . well, big and heavy. Many of us could not easily carry one on a day-to-day basis and, even if we could, we might end up causing problems for ourselves if we went about in mixed company with giant flashlights swinging from our belts.

Fortunately, there are smaller flashlights on the market that occupy every conceivable price range. We'll talk about the available technology presently. For now, think only in terms of size and application. Any small light is a cylinder of metal or plastic several inches long and about an inch in diameter. For our purposes, aluminum bodies are preferable for strength, though hard plastic lights will also do.

A multi-D-cell flashlight, heavy enough and long enough to be used as a club.

Much stronger than your articulated fingers and impervious to pain, a small light can absorb (and impart) force that your hand cannot. The small light is portable enough to be an item of daily carry. Because of the versatility and popularity of these little torches, they are the primary focus of this book.

These small lights come with multiple options for carry and transport. Many have built-in pocket clips, following the trend pioneered in the knife industry. There are vertical and horizontal sheaths available for those who wish to carry their lights on their belts. The flashlight industry is also replete with dedicated weapon lights for mounting to pistols, lights that fit into sockets on the end of expandable batons, and lights built into the plastic bodies of folding-knife handles. These latter items are not the focus of this book, but armed with the principles included herein you will be as prepared to use them as any other.

A clip-equipped tactical light rides in the pocket of jeans.

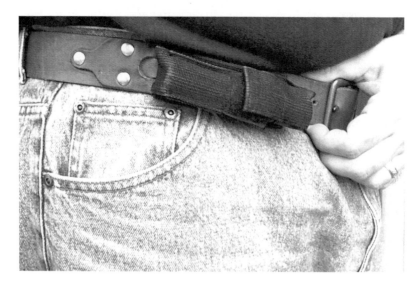

Horizontal belt sheath for a small LED flashlight.

Considering Lights

Chapter

2

The pace of technology is very fast; one could argue that technological development is moving faster exponentially. A new computer or other electronic device bought yesterday seems already out of date or overpriced compared to what we could buy today. Flashlights are no different.

While the conventional Maglite was once the standard by which all other lights were judged, it has been left behind by the current crop of ever-smaller, super-bright torches pumping out lumens in the triple digits. Because the market for tactical lights moves so quickly, we won't get very specific about the hardware. This book is about the principles of fighting with flashlights, which change little regardless of exactly how bright your torch may be. Your ability to defend yourself with such a tool is not directly related to the number of hours you can expect to get from one set of batteries, nor will it depend on whether the light produced is a true white or blue-tinted. These are details with which you can familiarize yourself when you buy your light, but they're just that: details. The principles are fundamental and apply across the spectrum of lights available. Learn the principles and you can adapt them to any tool.

As of this writing, there are three basic categories of portable torches on the market:

- Conventional lights range from the battery-powered plastic light my mother used to keep in a kitchen drawer, to my father's pen light, to the multiple-D-cell Maglites and a host of plastic camping and emergency lights on the market. They lack the blinding power of Xenon-bulb lights but are less expensive and are available everywhere.

- Xenon-bulb lights, as typified by the SureFire and Streamlight lines of tactical lights, are brighter and are becoming very popular. The type that uses two lithium batteries is comparable in brightness to a multiple-D-cell Maglight, but the bulbs burn out—sometimes just because the batteries were installed incorrectly. They really suck battery power quickly, too.

- LED lights, because they use LEDs rather than conventional bulbs, are sometimes "lifetime" lights—meaning that you won't need to replace the light source, but you will need to replace the batteries. There are many retrofit kits available for converting popular conventional torches to LED.

Are you bored yet? I don't know about you, but the specifics of the technology have never really interested me. I mention lumens output figures in this book for the sake of comparative figures, but I only barely understand what these figures mean. (I am unable to distinguish between *freaking bright* and *really freaking bright*.) There are entire Internet forums devoted just to flashlights, so if you're a

A small sampling of the many tactical lights in the author's collection.

real gearhead I would recommend joining one and indulging yourself. For self-defense purposes, all you really need is a light small enough to be carried daily. It should be bright enough when activated to be uncomfortable to the eye. There are countless tactical lights that meet this description. The only real technological consideration is the switch configuration.

For self-defense, you really want a light that has a momentary-on tailcap switch. A light with a twist-on head or a light with a switch inset on the barrel (body) can still be used as a striking tool (just as any cylindrical object can be used to hit someone), but they cannot be conveniently activated under stress.

The tailcap pressure button available on many tactical

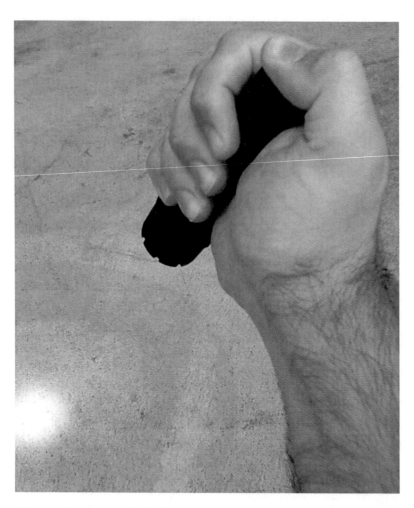

Tailcap switch on a tactical light.

lights activates the light when it is pressed. Releasing the switch extinguishes the light. Some switches produce always-on light when the switch is pressed more deeply, and some must be twisted for always-on mode. The important feature is that momentary lighting, which allows the operator to flash the light for only an instant.

The most fundamental principle of all low-light fighting is that sudden changes of light are disorienting. The loss of your night vision is the direct result of a sudden increase in available light. When you are suddenly plunged into darkness and your pupils are contracted for normal levels of light, the darkness seems total until your eyes have time to adjust. Momentary lighting produces those sudden changes of light and puts them under your control.

When you are facing an assailant in low-light conditions, your ability to suddenly flood his pupils with bright light gives you a very real physical advantage. There are no guarantees that you will blind him or sufficiently discourage him with light alone, but most people find the sudden transition from night lighting to, say, 60 lumens of Xenon-bulb torch light to be physically disabling for at least a fraction of a second. Most people instinctively flinch away from such bright light. Many will blink repeatedly while reflexively bringing their hands up in front of their faces.

I was puttering about in my study one day when I found a very bright tactical light—100 to 120 lumens—and started trying to activate it. I couldn't get it to work and was worried it was broken, not realizing that I had unscrewed the bezel for storage. I was staring straight into it, like a moron, when I screwed the bezel back down, zapping myself right in the eyeball.

"Gggaaaarrrgghhh!" I shouted. My wife, in the next room, probably wondered what the hell I was doing. I was temporarily disoriented and spent the next 20 minutes blinking away the green blob of the afterimage from that light. Up close in low light, triggering such a torch will give you a very real advantage against someone who is not expecting it. (Your mileage will vary if your assailant is on drugs or very drunk, but that's true of just about any technique involving pain.)

A friend of mine armed with a powerful Xenon light caused a drunken interloper to stumble and fall down by flashing him in the face with the light, completely shutting down his aggressive advance. (The same friend stunned an obnoxious moviegoer who was throwing candy in the theater. When he heard the punk whisper, "Hey, watch this," he turned and zapped the little bastard with the same light. The results were immediate, and the kid stopped bothering people.)

In low-light conditions, sustained lighting can also give you an advantage. Have you ever been stopped by a cop at night who flooded your car with light from his vehicle-mounted spotlight? Have you been stopped while on foot and had to talk to police or security personnel while they kept their Maglites on and trained on your face? Bright, constant light projected into your face isn't stunning or startling the way momentary light can be, but it is irritating, distracting, and often handicapping. Keeping your light switched on and focused on someone else gives you a distinct psychological and sometimes physical advantage. Be warned, however: some people react to such "light dominance" tactics by becoming more aggressive in order to regain the initiative. This escalates the confrontation.

A martial arts instructor I know was driving home from his karate school when he got into a traffic altercation with some sort of road-raging driver. The incident culminated in both of them getting out of their cars. My friend the karate teacher had a samurai sword in his back seat—something most of us would see as a major fight-stopper. "I'll bet that angry jerk was stopped short in his tracks when the karate guy pulled a sword," you might be thinking. Well, our road-rager wasn't just aggressive—he was smart. He got out of his car with a tire iron in one hand and a simple conventional flashlight in the other.

"He switched on the light and kept it trained at my face," the karate instructor told me, "and I couldn't see a thing. If he hadn't put it down later and then gotten back into his car to drive off, he could have waded into me swinging that tire iron and I wouldn't have seen it coming."

Your light, regardless of overall size and brightness, must be strong enough to be used as a striking tool. Most lights are up to this task, though you'll always run the risk of breaking it. I'm of the opinion that if I break my pocket torch on an attacker's face, I'll gladly retire the light and buy a replacement. (If you're successful in fighting off a would-be mugger using your torch, I'd recommend buying another just like that first one—and I'd frame the first light and hang it in my office.)

Small lights are not long enough or heavy enough to be swung like clubs. When you strike with small tactical lights, you're using them as pocket sticks—a means of concentrating the force of your blow (a hammer fist or a thrust). They can also be used as fist loads, which make your closed fist harder and stronger. (Very small lights that fit completely within your hand can only be used in this manner.) I saw a movie once in which a woman knocked out a man using a small but extremely heavy piece of gold jewelry he'd given her as a gift. The rigid weight in her fist put more power into the blow—something a small light can also do.

A very small light used as a fist load.

There are lights available with ridges, grooves, teeth, or other protrusions intended to make them more effective striking implements. The "anti-roll" facets on some lights are actually very effective striking tips. While there's no doubt that such protrusions do more damage when hitting another human being, they're also a potential liability. In court after the fact, a left-wing prosecutor (our courts are full of them, and they delight in making victims of victors) could successfully argue that you were looking for trouble because you were carrying a weapon. Keep this in mind when selecting your light. I own a few such aggressive lights and am not opposed to them, but I try to stay aware of the risks nonetheless.

Before we move on, I would again like to mention dedicated weapon lights. As of this writing, Glock manufactures a tactical light designed to clip on the accessory rails of its third-generation pistols. Other companies like Streamlight and SureFire manufacture similar items—some of which have cables and pressure switches for mounting on the firearm, and others with switches operated by the off hand while in a two-hand shooting grip. Many people find much benefit in owning lights of this type, but consider this: a portable torch can be used in conjunction with a pistol (there are many ways to hold the light in the off hand while shooting), but a dedicated weapon light is awkward at best when used by itself, detached from the firearm. If you buy a small,

Weapon light controls are activated using the support hand.

portable tactical light, you can use it for everything. If you buy a dedicated weapon light, you'll still need a small, portable tactical light to use for all your other needs. Postures and methods for using lights with firearms and other weapons are outside the scope of this text, but there is plenty of information available from Paladin Press on this topic.

Weapon light mounted on a pistol.

Using a light in the support hand while wielding a pistol for home defense.

Walk with Confidence

Chapter 3

Flashlight fighting is posited on the idea that the hand-held flashlight is a valuable force multiplier—a tool that does the same job in self-defense as does a lever in manual labor. A force multiplier makes it easier to accomplish some task by amplifying the power of human effort. The torch accomplishes this in three ways.

First, the torch makes it possible to see what is happening in low-light conditions. Something like 80 percent of all your sensory information is visual. Being able to see what you are doing is an invaluable advantage.

Second, the torch may temporarily distract or disorient an assailant. (You certainly can't count on this being the case, however, unless every mugger you face is a 9-year-old albino with an ear infection and the eyesight of Tolkien's Gollum.)

Third, and most important, the torch is a hard cylinder that concentrates force into a small area and is much more capable of withstanding impact shock than are the bones of your hand. *This* is the reason you should carry a torch. The other benefits are ancillary. By concentrating all your force on the tip of an aluminum cylinder you can hit someone much harder and with much greater effect than you could manage with your bare hand or empty fist.

Some critics will argue that holding a torch with one hand prevents you from grabbing with it or using it for palm strikes and other open-hand formations. This is true—just as holding an umbrella prevents you from playing the piano with that hand. I mean, come on—you have to be willing to trade something to get something. With a torch clenched in your fist, you can still throw any closed-fist punch you'd like—uppercuts, hooks, haymakers, hammer fists, vertical punches—and the torch becomes a fist load, bracing your hand and actually making it easier for you to punch harder. If you want to grab someone, you can simply drop the light to do it. Or you can secure the light to your fingers using a finger loop. (Appendix A describes how to use cord to attach such a loop to any flashlight.)

CARRY AND DEPLOYMENT

Before we get into body positioning and posturing, let's talk about carrying and deploying the light. You have only a few basic options. You can carry your flashlight in your pocket (or in a bag or other off-body location, though I don't recommend this), in a sheath on your belt, or simply in your hand as you go out and about. Some flashlights have built-in clips enabling you to attach them to off-body locations, inside your waistband, or inside a pocket. Many torches have lanyard holes or rings, enabling you to carry them using the lanyard as a wrist loop or necklace (though the latter is a bad idea for anything but small utility lights).

How you choose to carry your light is a matter of personal preference. Be aware, however, that the more secure the method of carry, the slower the deployment.

A light clipped to your pocket is very accessible and

always there when you need it, so if you can devote an entire pocket to this method, it's a good one. If, like me, you prefer to get some of your gear out of your pockets, you could go with a belt sheath. I prefer horizontal sheaths because they're more comfortable—but these do require the extra step of unfastening the snap or hook-and-loop closure in order to tug the light free. There are open-top holsters on the market, both bezel-up and bezel-down, made of leather or nylon. I have several nice friction-fit open-top holsters that I bought from Concealco (www.concealco.com) that keep the handle or the head of the light up above the belt line for an easy draw. Spec.-Ops. also makes a nice universal bezel-down sheath.

Concealco leather belt sheath used for bezel-down carry.

Spec.-Ops. universal bezel-down nylon belt sheath.

When I'm in a questionable area, I'll carry my torch directly in my hand so it's ready for use. If you're walking at night, it's a good idea to carry the torch anyway—you can blink the light as you cross driveways and intersections so nobody runs you down in the darkness. My daily carry light has actually saved my life, as I blinked it just in time to alert a driver turning into the driveway that I was crossing. Had I not done so he might have hit me, as he was moving much too fast for the neighborhood.

If you carry your light in a pocket or in a sheath, you must carry it consistently so you'll learn to draw it without thinking or flailing. I won't tell you how you must tote your light—just practice grabbing and deploying it until you can do it without difficulty under stress. You must integrate this draw with the proper body mechanics we'll discuss in the following chapter.

Identifying a potential threat and warning off the assailant.

Preparing to draw the flashlight while warding with the off hand.

Drawing the flashlight from a belt sheath.

Aggressively driving forward to strike with the drawn light.

Awareness and Body Mechanics

Chapter

4

AWARENESS

Before we can discuss body mechanics, there's something you must do. You must be *aware*. If you're considering carrying a torch for self-defense, that's great—but it won't do you any good if you don't also develop your awareness. Awareness is the most important component of self-defense. Only when you know what is going on around you can you possibly hope to deal with it. Only when you are capable of perceiving subtle (and sometimes obvious) cues in your environment will you have any hope of avoiding potential trouble before it becomes physical force directed against you. When you are out and about, you must make an effort to maintain a reasonable level of alertness.

This does not mean you must spend your days in a flop-sweating, trembling state of jittery paranoia. Rather, it means that when you are not someplace you can deem relatively secure—your home with your doors locked, for example—you must be prepared to meet physical force should you have reason to believe it is being offered.

When I am in public I do so in a relaxed but alert state, monitoring what is around me and assessing the behavior of those within range of me. If anything strikes me as unusual or potentially threatening, I pay closer attention to it, my awareness ratcheting up from baseline "aware" to "interested." If my interest reveals the potential for danger, I move to "on guard"—at which point I would start using body mechanics to establish and maintain my personal space in preparation for self-defense. (We'll discuss this at greater length shortly, I promise.)

When I am home relaxing, I lock my doors. I take off the considerable load of equipment I carry daily, from knives and my tactical flashlight to key rings, firearms, and other implements. I allow myself to feel safe. This does not mean, however, that I become complacent. I've made that mistake more than once and always regretted it. Just because you are home does not mean you can simply suspend your judgment, refuse to check out odd noises or other strange occurrences, or otherwise act like the world outside cannot affect you. I keep weapons and tools close to hand at home even if they are not on me. When I answer the door, I do so on guard. When I leave, I secure the place as best I can to prevent a break-in.

Once, not long after my wife and I were married, we lived in an apartment complex in one of those neighborhoods that is largely decent but slowly decaying around the edges. Late one weekend night, while I was asleep in the bedroom and my wife was still awake in the living room, an angry man started pounding on the door. It wasn't someone we knew; I think it likely that he was drunk or high (or simply enraged) and didn't realize he had the wrong apartment.

My lovely wife went to the door, looked through the peephole, and then went back to what she was doing. She didn't try to answer the door, didn't engage the intruder, and didn't deem it necessary to disturb me as long as he was only knocking. He went away as abruptly as he'd arrived, and we never saw him again. My wife told me what happened the next morning, and we agreed that she'd handled the situation exactly as she should have handled it. The would-be tough guy in me was a little disappointed that she hadn't come to get me, but that is irrelevant. She was aware, she behaved prudently, and we both remained safe at home.

Practice being aware. When you're in a restaurant waiting for your food, or waiting in line at the bank, ask yourself if you could describe the scene to a police officer. How aware are you of the people around you—what they look like, what they're wearing, and how they're behaving? When you're driving, ask yourself if you know the color of the car immediately behind you. Do you have any idea if there's even someone back there, possibly tailgating you? Is it a cop car? Awareness on the road will help you avoid accidents (and tickets). When you're home, maybe lying in bed just before you go to sleep, ask yourself what you hear. Are there any sounds, and, if so, what do they signify? Does anything sound unusual? Can you hear people or other activity outside your window or in adjoining rooms or structures? Once you strive to be aware of being aware, it will become second nature. You will be better off knowing what's going on around you. You'll have a better chance of assessing that it's time to deploy your light for action, too.

BODY MECHANICS

OK, now we're at the good part: the mechanics of flashlight fighting. Flashlight fighting is, for obvious reasons, centered primarily on the hands, as it is your hand that carries the light, and it is the light that inflicts the most damage. Lead with your hands and your feet will follow. You may study an art that focuses on footwork, and it's a good idea to practice moving forward and laterally, but we really won't complicate the footwork component any more than that. Keep your feet planted solidly on the ground and follow your strikes in to drive forward.

In order to do this, you must keep your hands up. The core of flashlight fighting is keeping your hands up to protect your head and neck, to keep your light on target, and to protect your personal space.

Whenever possible, it is while maintaining space—while

The "Jack Benny" stance is a good way to get ready to defend your personal space more aggressively without looking like you're doing so.

keeping our hands up to do so—that we'll do our flashlight fighting. The basic mechanics for maintaining space before deploying your light are pretty universal. I've seen the hands-up stance referred to as an "I don't want any trouble" position, a "fence," and a "de-escalation stance." Whatever the terminology, the basic concept is the same. When you are approached by someone who represents a potential threat to your person—be he a panhandler, a drunken barfly, or an incongruously aggressive stranger demanding the time—you must keep that person outside striking distance to avoid making yourself a potential victim. The first step in doing all of this is to get your hands in front of your body—inconspicuously at first, perhaps with a "Jack Benny" posture. From here you can put your hands out and start defending your space more aggressively.

The basic flashlight fighting ready position is a bladed (angled) posture in which the hands are up, staggered, palms open. This will look similar to many kinds of conventional guards and stances. The arms create distance and provide a protective barrier for your body (and, more specifically, your centerline, which is where you are most vulnerable). The body language is clear. It says, *do not come any closer*. The open palms are less aggressive than closed fists—and one may easily deliver strikes from this position, particularly chops and other open-hand blows.

You can combine your basic hands-up stance with appropriate verbalization tailored to the situation. It's amazing how effectively you can prevent trouble simply by saying, "Hey, man, I have the flu—you don't want to get any closer to me, I don't want to make you sick."

From the basic hands-up, palms-open, bladed posture, you have the option to deliver physical strikes if you must defend yourself. You also may choose to transition to your

31

Basic ready stance with the hands up.

light as a weapon (thus escalating the force used in the scenario). The most common justification for making this transition would probably be facing multiple opponents, in which case a weapon could be seen as a rational necessity on your part as the defender. (I'm not a lawyer, so don't take this as legal advice. It's safe to say that if you use a weapon in a violent altercation, you're going to have to answer for your actions in court.) You would also be justified in deploying your light if you determine that sudden

Aggressively warning the approaching assailant and preparing to draw the light.

illumination (in low-light conditions, obviously) might help you avoid inflicting further damage or that the torch would give you an advantage against a bigger, stronger, more dangerous opponent.

Light drawn and ready for striking.

What is this personal space that you hope to maintain? Your personal space is the range at which someone can touch you or reach you with a physical attack, such as a punch or a kick. Maintaining that personal space—guarding it against intrusion—helps prevent such attacks from succeeding. It establishes a barrier, a physical boundary, between you and the opponent. Whenever possible, do not allow people whom you do not know or do not trust to intrude on your personal space.

The Hands-Up Stance

Now, as we've discussed, keeping your hands up helps you maintain your personal space. Since I started advocating this method for dealing with being accosted, I've seen three major criticisms of hands-up ready stances and their use in space maintenance.

- *"Hands-up stances are too hostile."* Many critics see placing your hands up in front of your body as very aggressive body language and say it can escalate an altercation because it appears threatening. While it's true that assuming a double wu sao guard (a position from wing chun kung fu) or flaring your fingers into tiger claws might look like the prelude to a duel, the appropriate posture for maintaining space in flashlight fighting is much less hostile. With the hands up, palms out, combined with appropriate verbalization ("Whoa, there, friend, nobody wants any trouble, let's not crowd each other . . .") the combative nature of the stance is mitigated.

- *"Hands-up stances constrict your focus."* Some critics complain that a "fence" stance inappropriately focuses you on one person, prompting you to ignore or neglect potential threats elsewhere in your environment. While this is always a possibility if one is not mentally aware, it need not be a by-product of such a stance. You don't need to turn your brain off or stop scanning the area with your peripheral vision simply because your arms are raised. Even when dealing with a multiple attacker scenario, the greatest threat is presented by the person closest to you—*of course* you should focus on that person, at least initially. Just how many more ninja are hiding in the neighboring shrubbery is not your foremost concern; you must deal with the more immediate threat.

- *"Hands-up stances are vulnerable to grabs and breaks."* This is the complaint that always kind of irritates me because it shows ignorance of the way such hands-up stances are properly used. Hands-up stances are dynamic, not static. If you're standing there like a potted plant with your arms extended and unmoving, you deserve to have your fingers broken. The whole point of placing your arms in front of your body is to facilitate action and reaction. The second your would-be attacker gets close enough to grab you, you should be *doing* something. If he reaches for your hand or arm, that hand or arm should be moving, countering, hitting, or whatever you're inclined to do. It shouldn't be just hanging there.

Personal Space

We must pause now and leaven the theory of maintaining distance with some realism. In life, especially if your social interactions are healthy, you will find yourself in venues you cannot control. There will be times when you have no choice but to permit others to violate your personal space because the quarters are too close. If you've ever stood with others in a crowded restaurant or bar, waited in line at an amusement park, walked the congested streets of a major city, used public transportation, or even attended church, you have permitted others to get within striking distance of you. These situations are unavoidable. It is neither practical nor possible to lead a normal life while keeping every other human being beyond arms' reach.

When you must allow people into your personal space, your only choice is to remain aware of them and what they are doing. Stay alert but calm, absorbing what is going on in your proximity. If you detect something inappropriate, act on it. Until then, be content simply to watch or even feel those crowding you. There will be times when you are so crowded that you won't be able to look around easily; at those times your sense of touch (as others press against your arms and shoulders, for example) is your only indication of what is happening around you.

In self-defense scenarios, there will be those times when you cannot preserve your personal space. A sudden attack in which your opponent is abruptly on top of you is one such case. A seemingly innocent social interaction in which another individual surprises you through deception is another. You must be capable of fighting and of seizing the initiative even when taken by surprise. You will never be able to predict every conceivable situation in which something surprising could occur.

In those cases in which you do perceive a potential threat approaching and have both time and space to deal with that threat, you can employ the hands-up methodology. Keeping your hands up in the course of a physical altercation helps protect your vulnerable head and neck. Getting those hands up ahead of time provides that protection preemptively while helping to establish your personal space (and sending a strong nonverbal message to that effect).

OK, I'm going to risk boring you by repeating myself and emphasizing this in review. When approached by someone you do not trust, raise your hands with your body slightly angled, your hands open and your palms out. Combine this with assertive, nonthreatening verbalization—

something to effect of, "Hey, that's far enough, don't approach me, don't crowd me."

Combine your verbalization with movement. Step back if you must and if you have the room to do so; don't stay rooted to one spot. (Ideally, you want to keep moving forward once you're in self-defense mode, in order to gain and keep the initiative—but don't be afraid to give ground initially if by doing so you can prevent a problem altogether.) If the person by whom you feel threatened continues to advance, become more forceful. Warn your assailant verbally: "Do NOT approach me. I do NOT want you coming any closer to me. That is FAR ENOUGH." If the individual continues to advance on you despite these commands, he or she is aggressing; it is OK—if you deem the person a threat that justifies a force multiplier—to make the transition to your torch. Remember that when you deploy a weapon you are escalating the conflict. You must have legal justification to do so.

USING FORCE

You may or may not have time for all of the verbalizations described here, of course, because you may not have enough room to maintain distance between you and the attacker (who may be advancing quickly). When the individual approaches to within striking distance—the distance at which he can kick or punch you—you are out of time and you must preempt the attack. Be warned that YOU MAY ONLY DO THIS IF YOU ARE IN GENUINE AND CREDIBLE FEAR FOR YOUR LIFE. You cannot simply start driving a flashlight into people preemptively in the absence of the credible threat of serious harm.

The courts will use a "reasonable man" standard in evaluating your actions. A judge or jury will ask the question, "Would a reasonable observer share your opinion that an attack is imminent and you should be in fear for your life?" If those around you would not similarly judge the attacker's actions to be threatening (and sufficiently threatening to endanger you) then preempting the attack is not justified. You will be arrested and could be convicted of assault if you make such a mistake. Always judge your actions by the standards of a reasonable, impartial observer. Make your choices carefully, for you will pay for them if you are in error.

Generally, you are only legally justified in using parity of force. This means you can only use that amount of force necessary to stop the attack. You are not justified even to do this if the courts judge you could have avoided the attack altogether—meaning that if you can simply leave and avoid a fight, you are obligated to do so. You cannot use your torch if you know (and a reasonable observer would judge) that you can deal with the threat without escalating force. You cannot grind your attacker into paste after he's already neutralized; you cannot stomp him while he's down; you cannot take revenge on him for daring to attack you. You may only stop him from hurting you and then escape.

Attack, Attack, Attack

Chapter

5

Attack, attack, attack—come at your target from every possible direction and press until his defenses overload. Never give him time to recover his balance: never give him time to counter.

– Heroes Die,
Matthew Woodring Stover

From the hands-up stance, as your attacker (who has made his intentions clear through words and body language) moves into range, you strike him and overwhelm him using the basic torch techniques we'll describe in this chapter. When you're striking someone with a torch, you're using the concepts behind the pocket stick. Too small to be a true club and not long enough to extend your reach, the torch becomes a pressure tool that concentrates the power of the your blows into a much smaller, much harder area.

Whether you call it a pocket stick, a koppo, a kubotan, or a yawara, the operation of a rigid, handheld striking tool remains the same. Some people advocate using these stick-type keychains (and flashlights substituted for them) for joint locks and other compliance techniques, but these locking methods are too complicated for pragmatic street defense and too involved for the average person's use. We won't cover using the torch as the handle of a key flail, either, though many torches have a loop for a key ring. Flails, even when performed with a gigantic wad of keys on the end of the torch, simply aren't effective. A flail to the eyes has some value, but this is nothing you can't accomplish with a finger jab to the same target.

The techniques described herein are potentially lethal and could, at the very least, cause severe or permanent injury. When you use your torch to strike someone, you're using a weapon. You've escalated the force of the encounter if your attacker is unarmed. If you cannot justify your actions in a court of law, you're going to pay for them.

One last thing before we discuss striking with your torch. There will be times when, even though you are carrying a torch, you never get the chance to deploy it. Don't fixate on the tool. If you can't reach it and use it, you just can't—there's no law that says you must. It's a nice thing to have and it's great as unfair advantages go when facing unarmed opponents, but it is not a magic wand and it is not the solution to every situation. You've heard the saying, "When the only tool you have is a hammer, every problem looks like a nail." Don't treat your torch as the universal hammer for all problems.

BASIC STRIKES

I firmly believe the best way to use the torch as a weapon is with simple hammer-fist blows, delivered in rapid succession in combination with the off hand to guard and perhaps finger-jab as the light is driven repeatedly into an assailant.

The strongest grip is the simple clenched fist. However, since activating the light requires you to deliver strikes with your thumb capping the tail switch, this position increases slightly the danger of injuring your thumb if you strike an unyielding surface. You'd have to be striking very hard for this to be an issue, though, provided your fingers have a good grip on the barrel of the light.

You can also use a "pointer" grip for forward strikes.

Clenched-fist grip.

Using the thumb to activate the tailcap.

The forward strike is one in which the torch is held like a saber and used with a forward thrust straight into the target. The problem with this technique is that the grip is much weaker and the end of the light will be driven into your hand as you strike. Your light should have a tailcap switch, and a saber grip makes it difficult (though not impossible) to activate that switch.

Remember that your torch may or may not be long enough to stick out from one or both ends of your fist. If it is

Striking with the pointer grip.

too short to be used as a true pocket stick, it is still a fist load. A fist load is any hard item that braces the fist, regardless of weight. When you clench a small object inside your fist, you make that fist harder (essentially) and you make it possible to punch harder. (You might even increase the chances that you'll break something in your hand or wrist when you punch this way, but we've got to do what we've got to do in self-defense. Breaking something in your dominant hand is a pretty desperate trade-off for one or a few strong strikes, so be aware of the risk and don't take it lightly.)

When gripping a longer torch in the fist, it will project from one or both sides of your hand. The most powerful

Downward hammer-fist strike.

45

blow you can deliver using this grip is a downward hammer-fist strike. (You can also deliver upward blows if sufficient length projects from the top of the fist, but I favor the reverse strikes because they are stronger.) Those same downward hammer-fist strikes can be delivered laterally as backhands. You are striking using the tip of the torch to concentrate the power of your blows.

Lateral hammer fist (backhand).

Dynamic lateral backhand strike.

Those of you who do pikal knife jabs will find the mechanics of reciprocating hammer-fist blows extremely natural. Anyone with Filipino Martial Arts (FMA) experience will probably think it's intuitive, too. As you draw your light with your strong hand, your off hand comes forward to protect your body. As the light is used to deliver a hammer blow (overhand or as a backhand) it comes over or under the off hand and the two rotate each other as you ruin your attacker's day.

47

Reciprocating hammer-fist blows.

If you choose to trigger the light in low-light conditions while striking someone, you *might* gain a little by distracting your assailant. The greater the ambient light, the less this will be a factor, but the average tactical light is pretty bright and it's not something I'd want to stare into all day. If my pupils are dilated it might cause me some discomfort. Use your head. If you can deploy the light to your advantage while using it to strike, great.

The nature of the torch as a daily companion implies that you'll draw and use it from virtually any posture. I won't recommend specific modes of carry or draw beyond the options we've already discussed. Everyone's body style, clothing, and daily activities differ. Experiment and find what's comfortable and accessible to you. This isn't rocket science, after all. We're talking about finding a way to carry and draw a flashlight that isn't more than 5 or 6 inches long.

TARGETS

Now that we've gotten all of that out of the way, you're probably thinking we've forgotten something important. You're right—we've yet to really discuss *targeting*.

The head, face, and neck are the most vulnerable to flashlight strikes. Using your hammer-grip torch blows, you can drive the tip of the flashlight into the general zone of the eyes, into the cheeks, under the chin (and anywhere in the neck area), and into the hollow of the throat. You can also jam the light into an ear or into the temple, with varying results. Do what you must. Don't be afraid to put your flash-light straight through someone's eyeglasses, for example.

Strikes elsewhere on the body create varying degrees of pain and debilitation. I cannot guarantee that a given strike will "stop" an attacker, but there are a number of body-blow options. Blows to the side of the lower torso or to the armpit cause pain, as do strikes to the pectorals, to the biceps, inside the elbows, and to the gut. Kidney shots are unpleasant, too, as are strikes to the thighs, shins, and calves. Obviously, a shot to the groin will generate some notice.

When striking a grasping or grabbing limb—say, the hand or arm of someone poking you, grabbing your shirt, or reaching into your car—the backs of the hands are quite vulnerable, as are the areas of the arm inside the wrist and forearm. One technique used against a "bear hug" is to grind the knuckles of your hand into the back of the attacker's exposed hand. This is very painful with just knuckles but becomes even more so when grinding with a flashlight for leverage.

Also, remember that your hands-up stance is not a frozen posture. It's a dynamic means of maintaining your boundaries. When someone reaches for your limbs, move them—and react accordingly. Draw your light as appropriate and go to town on your adversary.

Remember: attack, attack, attack, as long as your assailant is still aggressing. Overwhelm him completely with a flurry of nonstop blows. Once he has faltered or even fallen, *get out of there*. Find a phone and call the police to report what has happened.

If your first instinct is simply to go your own way after the fight on the theory that if the cops don't know what you've done you can't be sued by anyone—think again. It's true that in our crazy legal system, people are often sued wrongly by those who've tried to hurt them and were injured in the process of failing to do so. However, if you are content simply to let a societal predator go his own way after vanquishing him, you reduce the chances that he'll end up in the system and then in prison. Reporting the crime gives the police a chance to link the suspect to previous crimes and put him away for them. (It's a fact that most societal predators are recidivists—repeat offenders for whom violence and crime are a lifestyle.) Weigh your decisions carefully and do the right thing. Always conduct yourself as you would if you knew you were being watched by a security camera—for in today's world, there's a very good chance you are.

PRACTICE

To practice using the light begs a little role-play. If you have access to a padded partner, so much the better. (I wouldn't recommend finding a friend and then pounding away on him with the end of a flashlight.)

I took some striking practice on the trusty Body Opponent Bag (BOB). Starting from a casual stance, you can move to a hands-up stance while using the appropriate, "Hey, nobody wants any trouble" body language and verbal de-escalation techniques. From there you can choose a point at which you must preempt BOB's attack. Teach his rubbery ass (well, OK, he hasn't really got an ass, but teach his disembodied torso) a lesson.

A typical application of flashlight fighting would follow this hypothetical progression from initial contact and escalation to defensive posturing and then preemptive or reactive striking with the torch. Here are a few more interpretations of how that might go:

You are minding your own business out in public somewhere when you are approached by someone. Let's say it's a stranger asking you if you have spare change. You brush him off, saying you don't. He continues to approach but is still outside of your personal space—the distance at which

"Whoa, there, BOB, I wasn't hitting on your air shield. She means nothing to me. Let's not get rowdy."

"That's far enough, BOB. Don't advance on me."

A flash of light to his eyes may disorient the attacker.

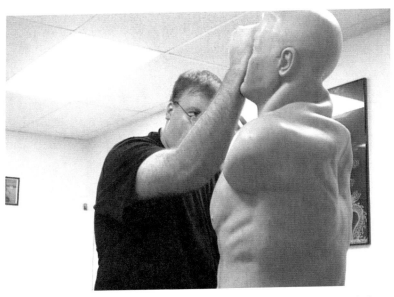

Follow the flash with repeated strikes to the face using the head of the light.

he could kick or punch you.

You raise your hands in the basic hands-up posture. You verbalize appropriately—"Hey, man, don't get any closer. I have the flu." He does not heed your warning, and you are forced to become more aggressive, saying, "That's far enough! Do not approach me!" He continues to approach.

He steps into range and raises a fist, shouting something incoherent and profane. You rightly judge, in that fraction of a second, that any reasonable person would perceive the threat of violence in your attacker's actions and words. You further judge that an escalation of force is appropriate to the threat. At this point, several different things could happen:

A) You step in and deliver a blitz of reciprocating hammer-fist torch blows to the attacker's face, rocking him back-ward. He staggers and falls down. You leave and report the incident to the police.

B) You pound a hammer-fist torch blow into his left pec-toral, causing him to falter for a moment. He puts his hands up and grabs for you. You keep your hands up, step to the side as his flailing limbs glance off your arm, and shoot a hammer-fist torch blow to the side of his head. He goes down, hard. You keep running in the direction you face in order to find a phone and call police.

C) Your attacker is faster than you. He throws a hook punch. You jam the hook with your raised arms, throw-ing a hammer-fist torch blow into the shoulder of the same arm. You drop your light as you grab hold of the back of the attacker's neck and shoulder and slam your knee into his groin repeatedly. He finally goes down and you flee to find a phone and call police.

D) Your attacker throws a punch at your head. You slap the

arm with your empty hand and then check it with the hand holding your torch. You flow into a pointer strike to his face. He covers but does not go down, so you stomp his ankle, then flee as he folds. You find a phone and call police.

While we're devising scenarios, here are two more:

You are downtown waiting to pick someone up. He or she is inside an office building and you are waiting outside on the sidewalk, next to which you've parked amid a line of cars. The neighborhood is not exactly a good one; there are plenty of people roaming the streets, talking and laughing, sometimes getting rowdy or posturing among each other when not catcalling to passers-by. What do you do? One potential response is to stay mobile, keeping a good cushion of distance between you and everyone else. I would recommend you draw your flashlight discreetly and keep it clenched in your fist, your arm held casually by your side. If you're fortunate, nothing will come of the situation; I have been in exactly that position many times when downtown and have not had to resort to force.

Now, consider the following. You are stopped at a traffic light with your window down when a would-be mugger or carjacker walks across the street and reaches into the open window, grabbing your arm. Having a flashlight handy could make a big difference, if you can grab it and grind it into his hand or wrist to make him let go. This is a difficult one because, if you're hemmed in by cross traffic or other vehicles in line with you, there is nowhere to go. It is difficult to exit the vehicle in that situation, too, as your attacker can surge forward into the opening door. Use your torch to pound any intruding limbs and floor the accelerator when you can.

A very bright tactical light is a great thing to have if your stopped vehicle is approached at night or in low-light conditions, particularly if the person approaching is a panhandler. Lighting up the beggar helps let him know that you're fully aware of his presence and anything he might try. At night, it can be disorienting to the person approaching.

As you can see from these scenarios, simply having a torch and striking someone with it can accomplish a lot—but it is not necessarily a complete system of fighting. You must be aware, you must be prepared to improvise, and you must be aggressive. Speaking perfectly honestly, I can tell you that arming yourself with a torch is only the beginning of acquiring the tools and skills you'll need for pragmatic street defense. To continue and to develop balanced skills, you need basic training in some martial art or defensive system (preferably a striking art), with cross training in grappling and ground fighting skills if possible.

The torch is a weapon that can give you a distinct advantage, but just having one isn't magic. You may own a gun, too, but that's no guarantee you'll never have to fight with your bare hands. With intuitive skills, some basic training in the martial art or self-defense system of your choice, and a little logic, however, you can add the torch to your arsenal and be well armed whenever you are out and about.

Chapter 6

Lights, the Future, and You

I have no doubt the pace of technology will continue to accelerate. If you're reading this long after the book has gone out of print, handheld torches are probably brighter and smaller than ever before. As of this writing I own one little regulated LED light that has a score of programmable brightness options, multiple modes of operation (including automated strobe features for Morse code S.O.S. messages), and so many instructions that they're printed on a wallet card—all in a light so small it can be completely hidden in my clenched fist. For all I know, there will come a day when manufacturers are producing lights so incredibly bright that tactical torches are legislated and controlled the way so-called "assault weapons" are today. Given that society is increasingly hostile to the concept of self-defense, you can bet it won't be long before we start to see rumblings from the Great Unwashed concerning why anyone would "need" such a super-bright flashlight. After all, such lights have no legitimate sporting use—do they?

It may sound cynical, but there's no getting around the fact that if you do successfully defend yourself—especially if you use your torch as a weapon—you're going to risk prosecution. If you're lucky, you'll simply live under the fear of prosecution for week after grinding week before the district attorney finally decides to let you off the hook. If you're not lucky, you'll end up in court, trying to justify your actions in front of 12 Monday-morning quarterbacks who don't understand force, who don't understand violence, and who think it's better to be a passive victim than an aggressive victor. It is not their fault that they believe this; they are programmed to believe it by our increasingly passive, increasingly helpless society.

Jeff Cooper wrote, of firearms,

> In my opinion, neither money nor greed (*cupiditas*) is the root of all evil. The root of all evil is envy. The non-coper hates the coper, and thus the non-shooter hates the shooter. I see no other explanation for the pointless and irrational activism of the gun grabbers on the political scene. They know that their machinations can have no effect upon crime. Guns have no effect upon crime, but they do make all men equal, as the saying goes. This puts the coper on top, and infuriates the non-coper.

Truer words have never been spoken. Your carry of a tactical light marks you as a would-be coper in a world of non-copers. While not nearly as provocative as a knife or a gun, the torch is nonetheless the tool of the prepared martialist—someone who believes in standing up for himself, in defending himself and his family, and in seeking every possible advantage in pursuit of success in self-defense. He is the antithesis of the pacifist, and he carries needed gear as appropriate. Among that needed gear is a good, bright, compact tactical light. As a martialist, the passivists and pacifists of the world will resent you. Understand this and understand that our legal system will work against you accordingly should you ever defend yourself (with or without a flashlight).

Why, then, would anyone choose to arm himself, to prepare for self-defense, knowing that society—large portions of it, at least—will hold one wrongly culpable for harming one's attackers? The answer is that despite the risks, many people understand that to live without fear requires us to be ready and able to use force. The old slogan goes that "it's better to be tried by 12 than carried by six." This isn't entirely true, and some people whose lives and livelihoods have been destroyed by lengthy criminal or civil cases might well tell you they wish they'd simply died.

It isn't the case, for that matter, that your choices are court or death. There is a lot of gray area in between—and a lot of room to make a mistake. If you are to go about your life without fearing every depredation, every insult, every infringement of your rights, you must be able to stand up for yourself. You must be able to assert yourself. If you are to do so successfully, you must be able to fight physically. There will always be those people willing to use unprovoked, naked force to settle a disagreement with you— whether that disagreement is over their desire for your wallet or their desire to abuse and humiliate you for fun.

Fighting encompasses a lot of topics—far too many to include in a single book on tactical flashlights. What you must remember is that a fair fight is no fight in which I ever want you to engage. A fair fight means your attacker has as good a chance to hurt you as you have to hurt him, all other factors being equal. I want those factors unequal. I want your fights to be grossly unfair in your favor. If someone attacks you, I want you to have every possible unfair advantage. I want the deck stacked in your favor. I want you to win, and I want your attacker to lose—and I want him to lose as quickly and resoundingly as possible.

Carrying a tactical light is just one thing you can do to be better prepared for self-defense. It is one thing you can do to cheat in the gamble that is self-defense. Remember, though, that while the handheld torch is a tool for multiplying force, zero multiplied by zero is still nothing. The person who makes self-defense possible is you. You will always be armed, light or no light, provided you understand how to use your brain. The fact that you've bothered to pick up this book is evidence that you're thinking—that you're using your primary means of survival and of self-defense.

Life is a struggle, but not a bleak one. In the journey that is to come, your active mind, your brain, will light the way to the choices you must make. It is your light in the darkness.

Use it.

Cord-Wrapping a Flashlight

Appendix A

One of the drawbacks to flashlight fighting is that holding a torch clenched in your fist prevents you from using that hand for anything else. This problem can be mitigated by adding a finger loop to your light, which will let you open your hand but retain the torch. Any cylinder can be wrapped with cord to produce a finger loop suitable for this purpose.

I first learned of this cord-wrapping method through my friend Don Rearic, who also made for me the first pocket-stick keychain I ever owned. What you wish to create is a finger loop for your middle and ring fingers. When your fingers are threaded through the loop, you can open your hand without dropping the wrapped torch. This is an extremely useful feature in a handheld tool, as it aids in retention while facilitating digital manipulation for grabs and grappling. You could even deliver an open-hand slap using the torch as a slapping surface. (I generally don't advocate this technique, though.)

There is no need to drill holes or to epoxy anything to your torch. All you'll need is a length of suitable cord, preferably paracord, which is available from many camping and sporting outlets. You will need something to trim the cord and a source of flame to seal the cut ends.

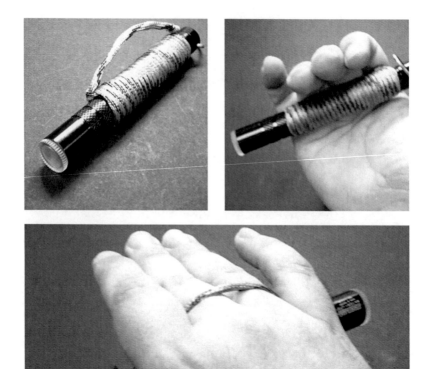

Cord-wrapped flashlight with finger loop.

CORD-WRAPPING A FLASHLIGHT

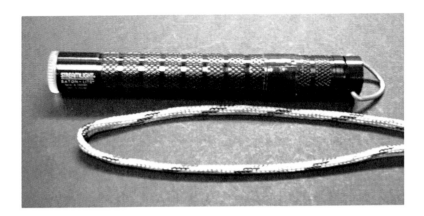

When wrapping a torch, I usually cut a length of cord about 6 or 7 feet, which leaves plenty of excess. Take the cord and make a loop at one end. Place the loop near the border of where the wrap will be on the body of your flashlight or pocket stick.

At the opposite border, leave a few inches that will stick out underneath the wrap at that end. Take the lion's share of the paracord and start looping it around the body of the light or stick.

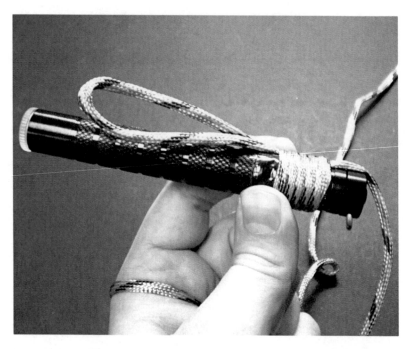

You're going to work your way slowly up the body in a tight spiral until you get to the loop you made at the first border. The trick is that you've got to get the loops as tight as possible or the wrap will be a mess (and probably be too loose at one end). If your hands hurt while you do this, you're probably pulling the loops tight enough.

When you get to the loop at the end, feed the cord under and through the loop and pull it taut.

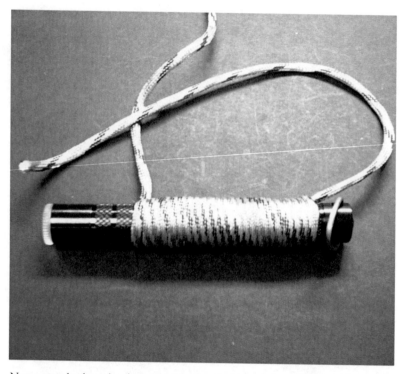

Now grasp both ends of cord at either end of your light or stick and pull with all your might to cinch everything up. Be careful to keep the cord loops lined up as you do this. The loop you made first should tighten up to constrict the long end, while—if you did this right—the cord bordering the shorter excess end will be tight too.

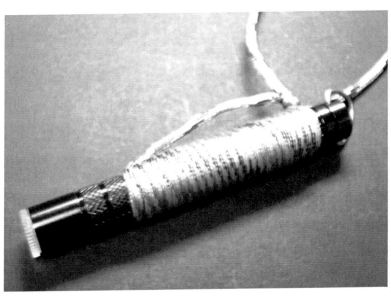

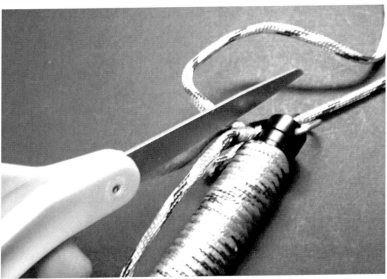

Now just size the loop to fit you, tie it off, and trim the ends. Burn the knot to seal it.

Larger Lights

Appendix B

Flashlight fighting is posited on the use of small, hand-held torches—lights ranging from keychain-sized fist loads to perhaps 6 inches long, give or take a little based on personal preference. This is because most people can't walk through life with multiple-D-cell Maglites swinging from their belts.

While larger lights are not the focus of flashlight fighting, there is no reason to ignore them. We'll run down the basics in this section so you'll be better equipped if you keep a large light on hand in your home, in your vehicle, or on the job.

A larger light has obvious fighting advantages over a small handheld-light. The two are not used in the same way for self-defense. We'll adopt as our standard the three-and four-D-cell Maglites. Filled with alkaline batteries (not rechargeables, which are almost weightless) these rugged, knurled aluminum tubes are heavy enough to be true clubs—and long enough to be wielded as fighting sticks. When I was a student at Alfred University in the early 1990s, the on-campus security detail was comprised of unarmed students wearing blue "Security" windbreakers. Their only weapons were large D-cell Maglites, but they still managed to do their jobs.

I once watched a pair of kali students run through a brutal pattern drill wielding dissimilar weapons—one student had a piece of steel rebar wrapped in friction tape, and the other had a multiple-D-cell Maglite. The ringing of metal on metal could be heard throughout the kwoon as they hammered away at each other. When they were done, the friction tape had been torn off the rebar in swaths, while the Maglite was scratched—but intact. Its bulb had burned out long before this test, so we weren't able to test its function, but that light held up under incredible abuse and more than proved its viability as a blunt weapon.

Any large, heavy flashlight can be used as a club if it is

Rebar and Maglite after fighting through a pattern drill.

The multiple-D-cell Maglite proved to be a formidable weapon.

strong enough to withstand the impact. Weight helps, but is not essential; a long flashlight can be wielded as in escrima and slashed into an opponent to great effect.

If you're at all familiar with the Filipino Martial Arts, you've seen (to estimate conservatively) roughly a million, billion, gazillion different pattern drills and sets of 12 to umpteen angles. Any of these can be applied to wielding the club, though a flashlight loaded with D-cells will be heavier (and thicker) than the rattan sticks with which FMA students practice.

To keep things simple, we'll use only the most basic angles—forehand (#1), backhand (#2), and a straight thrust (which we'll call #5 because that's the position it occupies in several of the patterns I've learned). The #1 strike travels straight overhand into the opponent's head or diagonally across the body, starting at the side of the head or neck and traveling across the torso. Picture slashing your war club *through* the opponent's body, cutting his torso diagonally in half.

I'm going to assume that you don't regularly carry a

Angle #1 strike diagonally across the body. The #2 strike travels back along the path carved by the #1 (it could also be a diagonal starting at the opposite side of the opponent's head and neck).

Angle #2 strike backhand along the reverse #1 path.

Angle #2 strike across the other diagonal.

Straight thrust, the #5 strike. The #5 is performed by stepping in and thrusting the end of your flashlight—the butt end, in most cases—as if you're trying to stab your opponent through the body.

light of this size. If you happen to have one within reach, the self-defense applications are obvious. Pick it up and start whaling the daylights out of your attacker using Angle #1 and Angle #2 strikes, throwing in an Angle #5 now and again if you're feeling particularly jaunty. The forehand and backhand arcs are generally easier to perform and very intuitive. Anyone can swing a flashlight like a club. Concentrate on striking your opponent about the head and neck, as blows to the torso are of less value. If you can solidly rap the assailant in the elbows, wrists, hands, knees, or ankles, do so. Break something if you can.

If you have occasion to square off with someone while wielding such a light but before physical force is initiated, hold it over your shoulder with the lens facing forward and projecting from the bottom of your fist. In this way you can bring the beam to bear on your adversary while in a perfect ready position for delivering an Angle #1 strike. You've seen cops hold their flashlights this way on television; they do it for that very reason.

One interesting development in the flashlight market is that companies like Maglite want absolutely nothing to do with the idea of their lights being used as clubs. They don't market them as such, and they want no part of any liability issues arising from an officer using one of their D-cell lights to club and possibly injure a suspect.

Thanks to the rapidly advancing technology about which I keep grousing, most D-cell lights are no more powerful (some much less so) than the current crop of super-powerful, super-small tactical lights. There is another cate-

Holding a large flashlight at the ready for a downward strike.

gory of (only barely) portable lights that we should discuss, however. These are the portable floodlights or spotlights that often come with vehicle adapters. I imagine such lights are used as often for jacklighting deer as for anything else, but they're extremely handy to keep around.

I once knew a self-described redneck from Ohio whose brother carried such a portable spotlight (with some ridiculous number of candlepower) in his vehicle. When someone approached him at night with high beams on, my friend's brother would "return fire" with the spotlight. (It's a miracle he never caused an accident.) Such lights are so large as to be unwieldy (most look like small beer kegs with handles affixed), so they're not suitable as physical fighting tools. Rather, it is the large volume of light they produce that makes them potential self-defense tools if you find yourself in a situation conducive to their use. I can think of one great example.

A good friend of mine is a truck driver. He is away from home on the road all week, returning to see his family on weekends. The rest of the time, he sleeps in his truck, parked at various truck stops. One feature of many of these stops is the presence of "lot lizards"—truck-stop prostitutes. A family man, my friend has no tolerance for such people and keeps a "no lot lizards" sticker on the window of his cab.

My friend was parked at a truck stop and preparing to turn in for the night when there came a loud rapping on the door of his truck. When he shouted, "Who is it?" he was greeted with, "Come on, Sugar, let's party." With the interior lights off, he peeked out the window and saw the hooker there. "I see you lookin', Baby," she said. "I know you want some!"

"None today," my friend shouted back. "Go away."

"Don't be unfriendly, Sugar," the hooker persisted. "Come on, let me in."

"No. I said GO AWAY!"

"I ain't takin' no for an answer," the hooker said. My friend wondered, at that point, if a friend or another truck driver had put her up to harassing him. He shouted again through the doorway.

"Look, if you don't go away, you're not going to like what happens. I'm not going to warn you again."

She started cursing him out, loudly. When she didn't go away, he took the portable spotlight he keeps in the cab, connected it to its power adapter, and put the light up to the window of the driver's door. The hooker—who had climbed up on the outside of the truck and was peering in—suddenly found herself staring down the barrel of that spotlight, which my friend triggered in all its eyeball-searing glory.

He told me that she fell off the cab and stumbled through the parking lot, clearly disoriented, swearing up a blue streak that was probably heard in the next county. I can only imagine that she must have been nearly blind with the giant green spots that were floating in her vision.

This was a very peculiar incident, and I don't imagine too many of you need a portable spotlight to deal with this specific problem. It's a fact, though, that at night or in low-light conditions, such a powerful lamp kept in a vehicle or a garage might prove very useful.

If you can stow a spotlight somewhere, I would encourage you to do so. I also encourage you to purchase a few multiple-D-cell Maglites and mount them in the company's excellent brackets. Under desks, in your car, on the wall next to the back or front doors of your house—there are many places keeping such a light would be very helpful. Spend some time brainstorming those times and locations in which you have wished for a powerful light.

Plan accordingly and watch out for the hookers.

About the Author

Phil Elmore is a martial artist and professional writer living and working in central New York. The publisher of *The Martialist: The Magazine For Those Who Fight Unfairly*, Phil has become widely known in the self-defense and martial arts communities. Frequently controversial and always opinionated, he has contributed articles to a variety of online and print publications. These include Paladin Press' popular collection, *Warriors: On Living with Courage, Discipline, and Honor*. Phil can be reached through his Web sites, www.philelmore.com and www.themartialist.com.